MOON CHILD RISING

Written by **Meredith A. Park**
Illustrated by **Frances E. Vail**

Inspirebytes Omni Media

Moon Child Rising

Text copyright © 2023 Meredith A. Park
Illustrations copyright © 2023 Frances E. Vail

All rights reserved. No part of this publication may be reproduced or transmitted in any form or by any means, electronic or mechanical, including photocopying, recording, or any information storage and retrieval system, without express permission in writing from the publisher.

ISBN Paperback: 978-1-953445-35-3
ISBN E-Book: 978-1-953445-36-0
Library of Congress Control Number: 2023934764

This book was responsibly printed using print-on-demand technology, in order to minimize its impact on the planet and the environment. Learn more at: www.inspirebytes.com/why-we-publish-differently/

Inspirebytes Omni Media

Inspirebytes Omni Media LLC
PO Box 988
Wilmette, IL 60091

For more information, please visit www.inspirebytes.com.

L.S. – You are my reason, my life, my heart.

I am your moon and you are my star.

Come with me on a journey
through waxing and waning.
I will guide you with my experience
and do some explaining.

I have been through the ups,
but sported many a frown.
And sometimes the hardest thing to do
was turn it upside down.

Some days are good, and some days seem bad,
but I find it best to focus on the better ones I've had.
I promise I'll be kind. Please know I'm always listening...
So, come take a walk with me, while the bright moon is glistening.

Today is the beginning of a new moon, you see.
Which means you could be feeling happy, or even feeling free!
You can soak up the sun and play all day long.

The illuminating crescent brings loads of sunshine, laughter, and joy…

Like the times you get to play with your favorite special toy.

Your body feels strong. You're full of happy emotions. Feeling so brave, you could explore all the oceans!

You can gallop with glee,
and spend time with your friends.
And at the end of the day,
watch beautiful colors blend.

Like a pie sliced in two halves, today the moon is divided.
Just think how much energy one-half has already provided!

From the tide to life-cycles, the moon helps it all.
It's truly amazing how it controls things big and small.

It's high up in the sky, always shining so bright.
And during its waxing transformation, it's like a glowing night-light.

Yet when you look at the sky and spy more of the moon, you know that harder days might be coming to you soon.

Your body can ache, and your head can feel foggy.
You can feel under the weather, or just a bit groggy.

On the harder days, you might curl up and cry.
And it's okay to let it all out with a GINORMOUS sigh.

Your body might feel like you just had a big fight. So ask for extra hugs and snuggle in tight.

The moon seems as big as the world, here on this day.
And you still may not feel like going outside to play.
That's okay! I promise, you will feel better soon.
Sometimes it just takes a few days and seeing less of the moon.

You might feel lighter and happier the very next day.
But you may need more rest before going back out to play.
Or, you might get a burst of energy, straight out of the blue.
But if you don't, it's okay, I'll still stay here with you.

Now your heart feels much happier, and your body can move.
You're dancing and shaking — getting back in your groove!

A weight has been lifted, and you feel more like YOU.
Now you can look at your journey with a clearer point of view.

Do you see half of the moon, up there? It's once more in the sky.
Go ahead, you can look. You don't need to be shy.
That great, big glowing ball doesn't need to cause you strife.
It helps nature thrive and supports all the planet's wildlife.

We are close to starting again, back at the beginning.

We made it through once more. See, the moon is now thinning.
From the North to the South and the East to the West,
be proud of what you've done. You did your very best.

You conquered your obstacles. You made the most of each day.
You did not give up, and you did not shy away.

Each day brings new hope, a new path, and new dreams.
And the moon is always there with you, sharing beautiful moonbeams.

It takes patience, self-care, and strength to keep going,
as you never fully know what the moon is bestowing.
Take what you've learned here, and never doubt what you feel.
Your struggles are valid and you deserve to heal.

Just remember this always, through both the ebb and the flow,
I will always be there with you, under the moon's glow.

I love you, my moon child. You are so brave and so strong.
The strength that's inside you has been there all along.

MESSAGE FROM THE AUTHOR

I created this story to help children with chronic health conditions—such as Lyme disease—understand that life, feelings, and symptoms are ever-changing. In our house, the phases of the moon guide us through our healing journey. There are good days and bad days, but there is always tomorrow. Embracing this perspective can help, whether you've been diagnosed with Lyme disease or are navigating another chronic health condition and diagnosis.

My daughter was diagnosed with Lyme disease at 19-months old. Our Lyme Literate Medical Doctors (LLMDs) diagnosed her Lyme as what is called congenital—meaning she actually got sick while I was pregnant with her. I have been sick for most of my life and only through her diagnosis was I able to finally find answers to decades-long questions about my own health. We have both come a long way and our healing journeys are not over. There will be many more challenges ahead for us but we will face them together, head on, and never give up fighting for our health.

Chronic illness affects not only those of us with the diagnosis, but everyone in our lives. There is so much strength within the community of chronic illness and I can promise you, you're never alone. Reach out, ask for help, and share your story. The only way to overcome the stigma of invisible chronic illness is to be an advocate for yourself and those you care for.

Whether you are just starting on your healing path or you have overcome obstacles you were told you never would; this book is for you. Whether you are navigating the medical needs of your child, a loved one, or yourself, I hope you can find comfort in knowing you never have to fight on your own. Hopefully this story finds a special spot on your bookshelf and is a reminder that you are always loved!

Remember, the moon will always rise... and so will you.

We'd like to extend a special thank you to the LymeLight Foundation for giving us hope and community when we needed it the most.

ABOUT THE AUTHOR

Meredith Park is a Lyme Warrior and mom who loves nature, photography, traveling, and spending time at the horse stable with her daughter. Her family is very important to her and Meredith is passionate about creating lasting memories together.

Outside of her professional work at an elementary school, Meredith channels her creativity in DIY projects and gardening. She cultivates happiness in her home by nurturing plants and caring for her pets.

Meredith has combined her love of storytelling with her passion for Lyme Disease Awareness and education to create her first book, *Moon Child Rising*. She is working on a companion book in which she hopes to share her journey with Lyme in order to help parents and adults navigate their own chronic Lyme Disease experiences.

ABOUT THE ILLUSTRATOR

As a child, Fran Vail spent many hours with a pencil in hand, practicing what would become her life's passion. Throughout her artistic career, Fran has worked in various mediums, including: watercolor, oil, pastel, acrylic, and ink. Her love for conveying image through form is unparalleled. In addition to fine art, Fran's volume of work includes: murals, architectural renderings, fashion illustration, private commissions, and children's book illustration.

With over 50 years as an artist, Fran has spent the past 25 years sharing her love for art through teaching. When not painting, Fran enjoys spending time with family and friends, reading, or attending art workshops in her beloved France.

ABOUT LYME DISEASE

If you think you or someone you care about has Lyme, contact a Lyme Literate Medical Doctor as soon as possible. There are many resources out there to help you on your healing journey. Ensuring you have reliable sources is key. Please consider the following websites when you begin your research:

~ LymeLight Foundation (lymelightfoundation.org)

~ Global Lyme Alliance (globallymealliance.org)

~ ILADS - International Lyme and Associated Diseases Society (ilads.org)

~ LymeDisease.org (powered by patients)

~ Lyme Disease Association (lymediseaseassociation.org)

~ Bay Area Lyme Foundation (bayarealyme.org)

"Lyme disease is an infection caused by the spirochetal bacteria–*Borrelia Burgdorferi*. If left untreated, infection can spread to joints, the heart, and the nervous system. Because the bite is painless, fewer than half of people with Lyme disease realize they have been bitten. Likewise, fewer than half of patients with Lyme disease recall any rash. Lyme and tick-borne diseases are prevalent across the entire United States with cases in each of the 50 states. The Lyme disease bacteria is powerful and has the ability to enter the brain less than 24 hours after a tick bite."
– LymeLight Foundation

"The CDC has announced that the number of people diagnosed each year with Lyme disease has climbed to approximately half a million, which is a jump of 59% over the 300,000 estimate previously listed on the CDC's website. This is based on new research in two studies in the publication Emerging Infectious Diseases."
– Bay Area Lyme Foundation

"Additionally, studies have revealed that Lyme disease can also be passed through the placenta of a pregnant woman to her unborn fetus, allowing Lyme to be a gestational disease."
– Lymelight Foundation

"The condition occurs when a pregnant woman infected with the tick-borne disease passes the bacterium, known as a spirochete, to her developing fetus. Cases of Lyme spirochetes crossing the placenta have been documented since the 1980s, with sometimes terrible consequences for fetuses and newborns."
– Mary Beth Pfeiffer, Author

"Patients with Lyme disease are frequently misdiagnosed with chronic fatigue syndrome, fibromyalgia, multiple sclerosis, and various psychiatric illnesses, including depression. Misdiagnosis with these other diseases may delay the correct diagnosis and treatment as the underlying infection progresses unchecked."
– Lymediease.org

"When detected in its early stage, Lyme disease can often be treated with an appropriate course of antibiotic therapy. If undetected and untreated, the bacteria replicates and the disease progresses into its late stages, becoming chronic. Treatment for Chronic Lyme disease is prolonged and complex. Patients often require years of intensive conventional and alternative therapies to fight the infection, recover immune function, and gain strength."
– LymeLight Foundation

Made in the USA
Columbia, SC
11 May 2023